T0131494

THE SAND
—— *between* ——
MY TOES

Ailsa Craig

BALBOA.
PRESS

A DIVISION OF HAY HOUSE

Balboa Press books may be ordered through booksellers or by contacting:

Balboa Press
A Division of Hay House
1663 Liberty Drive
Bloomington, IN 47403
www.balboapress.com.au
1 (877) 407-4847

Because of the dynamic nature of the Internet, any web addresses or links contained in this book may have changed since publication and may no longer be valid. The views expressed in this work are solely those of the author and do not necessarily reflect the views of the publisher, and the publisher hereby disclaims any responsibility for them.

The author of this book does not dispense medical advice or prescribe the use of any technique as a form of treatment for physical, emotional, or medical problems without the advice of a physician, either directly or indirectly. The intent of the author is only to offer information of a general nature to help you in your quest for emotional and spiritual well-being. In the event you use any of the information in this book for yourself, which is your constitutional right, the author and the publisher assume no responsibility for your actions.

Any people depicted in stock imagery provided by Getty Images are models, and such images are being used for illustrative purposes only. Certain stock imagery © Getty Images.

Print information available on the last page.

ISBN: 978-1-5043-1781-8 (sc)
ISBN: 978-1-5043-1782-5 (e)

Balboa Press rev. date: 05/13/2019

CONTENTS

DEDICATION

I would like to dedicate this book to all the poets out there; all the writers who have a story to tell or share. The time, the expressed feelings, the vulnerability of laying yourself bare at times, the shared moments, the sadness, the happiness, is often overlooked and not appreciated. Poets are the feelers; sensitive enough to situations to express emotions often felt by those who may read their words. There are so many wonderful writers out there who all have a unique style, some very deep and dark, others light and breezy and they all have a place in this world of words and thoughts because they all appeal to 'someone'. It takes time and effort to put a book together worthy enough to share with 'the world' of interested readers. Thank you for your effort and wonderful expression of thoughts found within your paragraphs of varied prose and poetry.

I'd also like to dedicate this to all the people who have wandered in and out of my life and inspired so many of my poems, given me courage to pursue my love of writing and supported me all the way. I wouldn't have persevered if not for their continual encouragement. Thank you so very much.

With love xx

Tides bring in life
then flow back out to sea
Time brings us life
then flows into our memory

- ailsa craig

INTRODUCTION

The sand between my toes represents the journey I have been on; the different shorelines of many stories and the footprints left behind. It represents the experiences that have stuck with me, even a few broken shells that have caused pain along the way. Some sand is course, some is warm and soft and some is difficult to remove but there is nothing like walking bare foot on the sand through life.

I have written many introductions for my poetry books and explained how my poems are, at times, messages that can drop into my mind at any given moment so I always need a pen and scrap of paper nearby to quickly write down my thoughts. I can be inspired by a song that will bring back a memory, a friendship that is important to me or a special love I have experienced on my journey, a beautiful view or place, and a moment in time. However, my poetry can also be inspired by others' joys and sadness and as I try to put myself in their position, I write the feelings that sweep over me at that time.

I find writing to be very cathartic for me; an escape into some sort of poetic reality that I need to release or an entrance into a world that fills my desires and warms my heart.

In the mainstream poetry of today, some of my writing appears to be very light or simple but know that where it comes from is very deep as I try to unravel the mystery of heartbreak, time, life and happiness mixed with the joy of adventure, friendship and growth. It is a part of me that I feel privileged to be able to share with those who open up my books and wander through the pages. Thank you for your visit along the shorelines of my thoughts.

A poet paints pictures
and takes you
into a world of words
that you either
relate to
embody
dream of
understand
love
disagree with
They are story tellers of
truth
hurt
pain
love
dreams
inspiration
adventure
imagination

A poet is a reflection of others'
woes or desires
A word said
A name dropped
A place mentioned
A feeling expressed or felt
An experience remembered
and from there
a poet writes

- ailsa craig

The sand between my toes ...

I've walked along countless shorelines
and felt the sands move between my toes
I've left many a footprint behind me
and lost more where the flow of the ocean goes
I've watched the sun rise and set
in places near and far
Kissed under the light of the moon
and wished on a shooting star
I've partied and danced with special friends
and lost my heart to a few
I've travelled to exotic places
and had an adventure or two
As time drifts quickly by
and I watch my children grow
I feel the years are getting less
to enjoy with those I love and know
So within my words are stories
some real and some just a dream
Some inspired by life's journey
or another's emotion depicted in a scene
One day my footprints will be gone
the sand no longer between my toes
The times of sunshine and laughter
will be left within my poetry and prose,
with love.

The hand of time...

I don't know
where the new winds
will blow
But I'll know
when it's time
time to go
I will see
the open road
I will see
the flight of the breeze
I will see
when I know
it's time to go

I don't know
if it's right
but the stars spoke to me
last night
and the moon
said to go
but I don't know
With the wind
at my back
and my past in the rack
I guess I'll know
that it's time,
time to go

I don't know
if the whispers
in my head
were from you
or life's ghosts
instead
I don't know
but yes,
I care
if it's time,
time to go

Can you hold my hand and lead me
for I know not what lies ahead
because I fear that it's time
as the clock of life once said -
You'll know when it's time,
time to go

Finding 'you'

The mask
fell
and there 'you' stood
A picture
of truth
Vulnerable
in the moment
Yet
more handsome
than I imagined

I could see
'you'
I had found
'you'

Your presence ...

Your voice is loud
even though I can't hear you

Your vision is so clear
even though our eyes haven't met

You feel sensual and warm
even though we can't embrace

Your mind is rich and inspiring
even though we don't converse

Your strength is strong and enduring
I feel you lift me when I fall

Your soul is so calm and peaceful
I feel your presence always nearby

Finding you, finding me ....

You'll find me in the silence
for that's where I roam
You'll find me by the ocean
a place in which I'm home
You'll find me in the mountains
on a rock perched up high
You'll find me in the clouds
as they gently layer the sky

Come find me in the silence
and venture into my mind
If I close my eyes and think of you
a vision of you I will find

Knight of the night ...

Who are you
the one who comes to me
when the lights go out?
I know you are here
I feel you
I am awash with you
The subtle movement of the curtain
though the night air is still
tells me of your presence
I feel you gently untousling my hair
as you sweep it out of my eyes
I see you looking down at me
such depth of emotion
as deep
as that reserved for those born
to me
Do I know you?
Were you a part of my past?
Are you a part of my future?
Or a part of a dream in which I exist?
I don't feel alone
when you are here
You make me wonder
but never fear
You are a part of the stars
a part of the moon
My knight in darkness
together again some night soon ...

Dear you ...

Trying to find the words to put into a letter.
Trying to find the words to reach into your heart.
Trying to see your face in the passages of my desires.
Trying to erase the distance that keeps us apart.
Will you read my message?
Will it reach into your soul?
Will the lines tie us together,
for together we are whole.
I hope my letter does find you,
wherever you may roam.
Then I'll know my words have found their path,
the path that leads to home.

With love …

The piano's music ...

The piano played
in the corner of the lounge,
the notes lingered in my ears.
Watching faces mesmerised
by the sounds
filling an empty space.
Thoughts drifting, intermingling,
as the music carried us all
to different dimensions,
different places in time,
different feelings felt.
Yet here we all are sharing the same
special space,
filling it with so many thoughts;
each one with their own notes,
their own interpretation –
making a beautiful symphony
of life.
As the piano played …

Carousel of life ...

Life is like a carousel
we have choices as to how we ride it.
We all get a ticket and if we don't like our first choice
we can change the ride.
Do I get on a horse?
Ride with the wind in my hair,
feel the freedom as we gallop through life
over the various plains before us.
Do I ride a fish?
Follow the currents,
let them guide me from shore to shore,
stay with my own tribe not knowing when temptation
may hook me and take me away from the familiar.
Do I get in a swan?
Be graceful and a thing of beauty,
create a vision worthy of admiration,
pleasing to the eye of appreciation and
content in my lake of life.
Do I get in a cart?
Let someone else take me wherever they lead,
just sit back, enjoy the ride but never quite knowing
where I am being taken to.
Do I hop on an elephant?
Knowing my strength will get me through life,
slow and steady,
loyal and protective to those who have shown kindness
and friendship without expectation.
Whatever the choice, there is no right or wrong.

Wherever the ride takes you,
You are part of all that life is
and all that makes it a colourful,
interesting ride to enjoy -
on the carousel of life,
however long your ticket allows you.

Oranges and lemons ...

Oranges and lemons all in a row
How did I get here
I don't know
I watch from my window
knowing all too soon
I'll watch the cow
jump over the moon
I'll sit here and wonder
what I have seen
How did the vine grow
so big
from just one bean?
Childhood days
fade into the haze
as stages of life come to a close
and I sit here and reminisce
writing sweet memories
in prose.

Shooting star ...

....and there you go
I didn't get the chance to know
who you are
I just noticed your star
so I made a wish
and closed my eyes
but it came as no surprise
there was no reprise
of my moment
with you

The driftwood....

Drifting
in and out of sense
washed up
on a shore in unreality
Lying here
not knowing where
I am
(on a soft bed of sand
with the taste of the sea)
A piece of me remains
drifting
here in a place of indifference
If I am
found
I will find my
reason
and drift back to the shore
of reality

You are unique ...

Tip toe through life
but always make a sound
Tip toe through joy
wherever it may be found
Tip toe through love
and enjoy all that it can bring
Tip toe through kindness
make other hearts want to sing
Tip toe through daisies
that flourish in the field
Tip toe through others' hearts
make sure it's love that you do yield
Tip toe through magic
let sparkles make you glow
Tip toe through life
wherever you may go
Tip toe gently
but make your presence felt
Tip toe with confidence
and many hearts you, no doubt, will surely melt.

Urquhart Castle

Haunted mist of
time before
encasing castles
on the shore
Whispers of the past
swirling around within
seeping into the memories
of familiar visitors and kin
Still standing proud
outlasting its foe
Time cannot destroy
all its history to us
the castle does bestow ...

Flow of life ....

Carried within
the ripples
of the river
are
ghosts of time
drifting
and caught
in the currents
of life
merging into
the vast ocean
of past souls

Voice in the clouds ...

Do you hear me call
from a distant place
My words written in the clouds
swept away without trace
Do you see me
standing here
A mere speck
in another hemisphere

Life plays games
as we are dropped through
the sieve
Learning to share each day
with those we can't give
our hearts to ...

Floating through life ....

Like an empty vessel
floating on the sea
No wind in my sails
guiding me
into the blue
of infinity
where I will find
my liberty
The seas are calm
waves roam another shore
I look to the stars
guiding others once before
But with no oars
in use
and no place to reach
This empty vessel
floats
until it finds its niche …

My days without you ...

Kind smiles stare in vain,
trying hard to erase the pain.
Lovely hearts made of gold,
warming a sadness growing old.
I miss your presence in my day,
you put a reason in the words I'd say.
Now my sentences are standard issue,
as I reach for another tissue.
Miss you my friend

Love's connection ...

As I walked through
the winter mist
I knew you were near
when I felt your kiss
Our thoughts are always
joined in time
Our connection strengthened
with love's eternal twine ...

Life and time ....

As we wander along our path
in time
and share our life with those
in line
I'm so glad with those who share
their time with mine
sometimes pausing when we reach
a sign

Some just saunter
and enjoy the view
Some race through life
dodging the queue

I wonder what life is like
a hundred years on
when we're just a name
on the family tree we belong

Time is just a moment
we mark it with clocks
Sunrise and sunsets
until our boat docks

Her wave ....

She rose to a great height
then tumbled with glee
into life
She spread her bounty
for all in her surrounds
to enjoy
until all she had left
was a mere trickle of
her original self
Could she gather all that
made her what she once was,
her spirit, her strength
and once again dance with
the chorus,
within the ocean of life …

His gaze ...

She didn't realise
how lost she was
until she got caught
in his gaze
and found
her way
home

Music of the waves ....

When I see the waves roll
I hear music in my soul
singing songs of long ago
The ocean seems to know
of the memories
each wave sings
and the joy to me it brings

Who knows what one day will bring ....

Will it bring us sunshine
Will it bring us rain
Will it bring us happiness
Will it bring us pain
Will it bring you back
Will it take me forward
Will it bring a sign
A horizon to walk toward
Who knows what one day will bring
We live our lives hoping one thing
that we find a way,
a path,
that takes us to this day …

Forever free ...

The grasses gently sway
to the sounds of the ocean breeze
They drink in the flavours
of the sea
and colours of the sand
I feel you in their motion
like you are dancing to
our tune
Your presence is everywhere
in all the beauty I see and feel
Your spirit is like the endless
wave of the ocean –
forever wild and free

In the moonlight ....

When the light of the moon
shines at night
I see your shadow
standing in the light
You stand and watch
from across the seas
You watch when life
drops me to my knees
You watch as I too
stand in the light
and pray your soul
will hold me tight
And as the sun
shines on the morning dew
I give thanks to life
for bringing me to you

Unchain me ...

The bells kept ringing
that's all I could hear
In the darkness outside
there was so much to fear
I had hidden before
tried to escape the routine
but the bells kept ringing
and no daylight was seen
I tried to call out
I banged on the door
I couldn't see in front of me
only where I'd been before
I knew there was a reason
I had to find a way
but the coldness that surrounded me
locked me in the night of the day
The bells just got louder
they were all I could hear
so I hid in the darkness
daylight must be so near
I must fight the sound
I must fight the fear
I must unchain yesterday's sadness
and then the darkness will clear

Goodbye ...

Time and tides
have taken
you away
into my yesterday

A moment of magic ...

In the glow of the light
which shone through the night,
into my sight,
there I saw a fairy.
With her hair of gold
and her wings in fold,
rarely seen I'm told,
she looked up at me.
She smiled so sweetly
as she sat on the branch,
she looked straight into my heart.
I felt my body lift
as though I had wings,
I didn't want this moment to part.
She reached up to me,
in her hand was gold dust.
She then blew it towards me
and said, "You must let in trust.
Be unafraid of what you see.
Be unafraid of what you feel.
When you listen in silence,
think of the magic of seeing me.
I am here for a reason
and so it seems,
I want to lift up your spirits
and guide you to your dreams."

The hue of you ....

Rainbow trails
seas of pink
White sails
in the sunset
Makes me think
about when I
opened my eyes
and saw you in the hue
It came as a surprise
I wasn't expecting you
to colour my world
as beautifully as you do

If I give you ...

If I give you my hand
where will you lead me?
Will we dance through the clouds
or sail across the sea?
Will we explore distant lands
and look for buried treasure?
Or climb the highest mountain and discover
our true pleasure?
Will you sing me songs
and pull me in near,
don't let me go,
don't leave me with a tear.
If I give you my smile,
I will give you my hand,
please hold it tight
as we venture to our new land.
If I give you my hand,
I will give you my heart.
Always together,
never apart.

Into you ....

One day I tripped and fell into
your eyes
but here I felt no fear
for within your eyes and beautiful soul
it was a blessing to just disappear

One day

One day
the gift that I so long for
the gift I fear I may not receive
will one day be
the realisation
that I was surrounded
by it all along
It may not be the intense
desire
written by poets and musicians
or played out in love stories
but it is there
it is real
it surrounds me
everyday
in family, in friendship, in connections
in everyday life
the gift
I have received over and over
One day
one touch, one smile, one word
will be enough
for me to realise
I am loved

Maybe

Maybe if the sun will shine
for one more day
Maybe your shadow
will stay behind the warm yellow ray
Maybe then I'll believe
in fate
Maybe life will unlock the gate
Maybe when you walk my way
maybe your look will make my day
Maybe will then no longer be used
as once again our hearts are fused
together

Murky waters of murky words

A river of words
flowing
from mouths with many accents
Flowing
collecting others as it flows
Words of thoughts
- born out of ignorance
- born out of pain
- born out of hatred
Flowing
building momentum as it flows
and turning the river
into a murky darkness
full of mud ready to sling
at unsuspecting comments wandering by
Innocent remarks of concern
regarding the build-up of dirt
in a river once noted
for its beautiful clear waters
of understanding
of freedom
of respect
of difference
as it wove its way
through the many diversities
of life
Once upon a time
once when words flowed

and were used
to mend broken lives
to bring together and celebrate
our differences
The river of words
flowing
(it's up to us to stop the pollution)

Lonely voices

Lonely voices make no sound
Silent footsteps on undiscovered ground
Eyes that see but cannot focus
Disappearing moments like hocus pocus

Unimagined sadness
as she watched life walk by
No one knew the smile she gave
hid a tear in her eye
She felt such a burden
to all who held her hand
It was hard to explain
what she couldn't understand

Lonely voices make no sound
Kind ears are hard, at times, to be found
Eyes that look through darkened glass
watching precious gifts fade
into the past

The pathway

If I wander through
the garden
the garden of your mind
I'd pick a wild flower
and press it between the pages
of my heart

If I wander along the shoreline
the shoreline of your ocean
I'd find a beautiful shell
and put it to my ear
just to hear your voice

If I climb a mountain
a mountain of your strength
I'd find a hidden pathway
that leads to your soul

and there I would find
peace

My blue bird ...

My little blue bird
fly high
Please carry my message
safe within
your wings
Fly and be free
and rest my message
in the clouds
above the home of my heart
so when it rains
my words will fall
like raindrops
and bring life to the seed
planted
once upon a memory

Rainfall of tears

Don't let the rain fall
be the reason for our tears
Don't let the days we lose
turn into years
Don't let our memory
just fade with time
Don't give your smile away
it blends so well with mine
How can I look at another
with you tattooed on my heart
How can I not think of you
we connected from the start
Don't let the rain fall
be a reason for my tear
Don't let the days apart
be a reason you aren't near
If I could work out
how to fill my space with you
my life would be in heaven
because you are all to me that's true

The nightmare

She lay there
comatosed –
frozen in a state of panic
She let out a silent scream
unable to vocalise any sound
Fear gripped her heart tightly
as her breathing struggled
to maintain momentum
She was completely imprisoned
in her nightmare
until
her eyes focused
the darkness dissipated
as the morning looked through
the window
Light battled the darkness
Her limbs gained mobility
She had escaped the dread
stalking her dream
She rose to greet the dawn
free from her captor
free from her fears
free to fly again
into the light of a new day

Such a gift ...

The adventure in your soul
is so exciting
The gentle care of your touch
is so enticing
The giggle in your laugh
is so contagious
The cheekiness in your grin
is so enchanting
The concern in your heart
is so beautiful
The honesty of your character
is so trusting
The art of your conversation
is so inviting
The strength of your commitment
is so rewarding
The love in your eyes
is so illuminating
The sincerity in all who you are
is like a breath of fresh air
You are a gift that just one word
can't describe

The nature of us ...

Some people are like the stillness of a calm ocean –
very peaceful to be around
Some just make you smile or laugh –
really uplifting to the soul
Some bring the wonder of imagination,
colour and adventure into your world
Some just make you realise, it's good to be alive –
conquer humdrum with excitement and motivate you
to 'dance', to take on the world
Some are like a wild, stormy night, instilling
fear and an unsafe atmosphere to be in
Some carry the weight of the world within
their whole demeanour and bring a 'heaviness'
into your space
and then there are those who bring a little bit of everything
with them and you never quite know
what mood awaits you
We are all part of nature –
The moods that surround us
also dwell within us
depending on what stimulates
whichever reaction
the nature of us
responds to

The embrace of your words

As I read your poetic words
they seem to come to life
and dance on the page
They are entwined together
and flow so gracefully
It's like your hand reaches out
and pulls me into an embrace
within your words
I feel every syllable as it
touches me with the gentle stroke
of your pen
I am mesmerized by the dance
as I swirl around happily
ensconced in the magic
of your story
you have so beautifully
imprinted
on the page before me

Sweet river ...

Sweet sweet river
flowing through the night
Sweet sweet river
watching the grace of swans in flight
If I should ever follow you
will you carry me with care
Sweet sweet river
our hearts will meet somewhere
Sweet sweet sunshine
warming up our day
Sweet sweet sunshine
watching palm trees sway
If I should ever need you
will you reach out your loving hand
Sweet sweet sunshine
ours hearts will meet in wonderland
Sweet sweet rain clouds
covering our skies in grey
Sweet sweet rain clouds
peaceful sounds of rain drops at play
If I should ever seek a safe haven
will you guide me with a song in tune
Sweet sweet rain clouds
our hearts will dance 'neath the light of the moon

I sense you ...

As I wander through my mind
I find a place to sit
and contemplate
the feeling of you that brought
me here
You are here with me now
The sense of you is so strong
I slide down your smile
and rest
on the softness of your lips
I could stay here forever
Then I follow the outline
of your face until
I am drawn into
the magic of your eyes
They sparkle with such intensity
I just want to marvel at
their glow as they flow
into
and illuminate my soul
I can always feel when you
are with me in our thoughts
and I so enjoy
having you visit –
whenever
you wander
into my mind

Come visit ...

I can only wish
that within the light
of tomorrow
you appear out of the shadow
of yesterday
and appear before me
on my pathway
and into my smile zone
once again

I miss sliding down
the curve of your smile
and landing in the blue seas
of your eyes
and just floating there
for awhile

Love heart ...

Can I write you a poem
wherever you are
Whether you roam this earth
or on a nearby star
I know you exist
your light shines so bright
You are worthy of words
don't hide in the night
Those who can feel you
sense when you are around
Your heart is immense
Your voice makes no sound
You are in kindness
You are in a smile
You share a part of yourself
every once in a while

This last verse is hard
to summarise all you give
You are the beauty of love
and
you make each day easier to live

Innocence of nature

The innocent scent of the wild flowers
overwhelms my senses
The hills are painted with splashes
of their colour
as they roam
like free spirits
no boundaries
to contain them
The lake at the foot
of the hills
is imbued with all the shades
of blue
and so clearly reflects
all that surrounds me
The beauty I find myself in
carries my soul
to a place in infinity
as it wanders
through nature's
moments
of breathtaking
artwork
and blends into
a feeling of complete
serenity

My dear friend

When I write about you
I feel you close again
as if you are standing
looking into me
and smiling
Yes
looking into me
The intensity of your eyes
spoke volumes
only we could understand
You brought a beautiful something
into my life
A something I have never really
been fortunate to feel
I thought I had but now I realise
what has been missing
all this time
and what I probably
won't be gifted again
I guess there was a reason
you stopped and waited for me
that day
and I guess there was a reason
you had to leave
and I understand
because
you were a niceness
that blew into my life

and brought a smile of sunshine
and eyes as deep as the ocean
and a heart so sincere
it had to move away
Maybe in another time
another life
you will stop and wait for me
again
to catch up
and this time
there'll be no more
goodbyes
This time
it'll be as it should be
Until then, my sweet friend

Adieu

Farewell to you ...

Time to whisper
a soft goodbye
Don't look too close
or wipe the tear from my eye
I can't hold on to all that
I feel
It's time to let go
and return to what's real
I will miss you

Highlands

I want to wander
through your valleys
and feel the history
of your soul

I want to climb
your snow-capped mountains
and feel your strength
envelop me

I want to bathe
in your deep blue oceans
that drown me
in your moods

I want to feel
your breezes swirl around me
as you playfully
tangle my hair

I want to sit under
the stars of your night
and know that
I am home

The devil in you

When the devil comes to town
those in know, sense a fake crown
You wear it with such pride
but there's pain deep inside
You think by taking what's not yours
will open some self-satisfying doors
But until you heal that pain
taking smiles from others is not a gain
for the hurt that you do bring
is a song only the devil knows how to sing

So when the devil comes to town
jump off your high horse
find a quiet moment
and calm down

A love story ...
(Dedicated to my parents)

You have seen each other
through the wrinkles of time
You gaze into each other's tired eyes
and see the beautiful person
you first laid eyes on
and smiled
You see the person who made you
lose your voice
when they came near you
You see the person who loved you
intimately
with passion and desire
You see the person who, with you, together
produced new life to love and share
You see the person who's been beside you
through all your ups and downs
You see the person who loves you
like no other
You see the person who nervously
placed their hand in yours
and has never let go

Through the wrinkles of time
your love story
has grown
An eternal love story
you have written together

Always with you ...

(For my children and theirs)

I wish I could hold your hand
and walk with you through life
There are many years in front of you
may they be happy and free of strife
I wish I could protect you
from many horrors in life these days
There are some cruel and evil minds around
who make life like a trip into a maze
I wish I could just make sure
that life treated you well
There are many hurdles to jump over
and rivers beginning to swell
Know that I am with you
and will do all I can to make sure
that you smile each day you walk this earth
until your ship finally sails from shore ...

Life's daily performance ...

Buses on the street
Footpaths pounded
by many different feet
Buildings so tall
they touch the sky
Workers on top waving
to travellers flying by
To and fro
the people march
some beefed up with protein
some enjoying starch
Some with smiles
they love their life
Others are sad
and may even face strife
All of them stories
each day is a new page
The theatre of life
performing our chapters on stage
Buses on the street
Cars driving by
Our lives are amazing
without really having to try

Wyatt

Trucks and tractors
planes and bikes
Just a few of the things
this wee lad likes
He'll climb whatever
as long as it's high
You can't look away
you just gulp and sigh
His smile is sweet
His eyes are blue
His cuddles are so warm
when he has time for you
He loves to explore
and enjoys a snack or two
He'll always melt your heart
when he looks at you

For Milla ....

There is a little girl
who's as sweet as a honey bee
Her eyes are as big as dinner plates
and the colour of the beautiful blue sea

Her lashes are long and gorgeous
her mouth like a cupid's bow
She can stand her ground
if you upset her
So mind you don't stand on her toe

She makes up cute little stories
about fairies and princesses alike
They go on amazing adventures
and she'll take you along for the hike

She's a lovely little sister
with luscious long brown hair
She's as pretty as a picture
and will no doubt attract a fairy prince's
stare

Willow

Little tears in eyes
of blue/green
well like pools
on a face so serene
Slowly they fall
down cheeks tinged with rose
Like a sad waterfall
they roll past your nose
Your sweet little face
looks into mine
and my hearts bursts
as I say goodbye
one more time
The smiles you give
are certainly made with gold
You are a beautiful old soul
even though you are only
six years old

Can you see me ....

If I look out in wonder
far over the seas
or run through grassland
covered in daisies
If I hook onto a star
or fly to the moon
or sing you song
on a stage in your room
If I trek across mountains
all covered in snow
or dive to Atlantis
the city way below
Will you notice that I'm not
one of the crowd
even though my voice
is not very loud
If I look out in wonder
far over the sea
will you sail into my dream
and come rescue me
You are special to know
Your heart shines through
in all who you are
and in all that you do

The quandary of you ....

Some days are sad
thinking of you
Some days are happy
thinking of you
Some days are hard
knowing you are gone
Some days are special
knowing you came into my life
Some days tears fall
I miss you
Some days tears fall
you make me smile
Life is what it is
Life is lonely
Life is full
Life is different
You are somewhere
Life is life
I will find you
where the smile
meets the kiss
and whatever follows
Tears will turn to bliss
and I will find you
once more

The night of her journey ...

As her eyes closed with the tiredness of the day
she felt her soul drift on the clouds
of her dreams
She lay on the wings of a dove as it carried her
through the mists of time
to places and people once visited
once shared smiles with
once loved
She felt the desire to let herself fall back
into a time and space long gone
but she couldn't let go
It was as if
she was the bird's wings and had to keep
flying
floating
looking but not touching
remembering but not going back
The clouds covered her in a misty moisture
like an accumulation of all the tears shed
for all the feelings felt in the place
of her memories
But as she looked ahead, she could see
the magical colours of the rising sun
She could feel the pull of a new day -
a new tomorrow waiting for her
Waiting for her to experience –
to love again
to laugh again

to be herself again
Her journey though life was still evolving

Her flight on the wings of her dreams
gently placed her in the arms of a new day
with you

In one special moment ....

One morning
One night
One day
One year
One sunrise
One sunset
One rainstorm
One sunny afternoon
I met you
I met you

and time stopped
for awhile
and then the world
turned upside down
and it all made sense
because
I met you
I met you

The signs

Wander through the sunlight
of your soul
Gaze at the stars that shine
in your eyes
Capture a moonbeam
in your hand
Let it guide you
to my smile
and know the love that
keeps my heart
beating
is for you

Loving you ...

A heart full of love
has
a beat full of flutters

Cheeks tinged with rose
in your presence
A smile radiates
a familiar glow
and
nerves tingle
with thoughts of you

An invisible magnet
draws us in
close
Eyes are locked
in one direction
A warmth I feel
whilst in your arms
A coldness surrounds me
when you're far away

Makes loving you
an enchanting adventure
to be on
and a beautiful time
we share together
I love you

You have never left me ....

You reached out through
time
and touched my soul
I saw the moon smile
and the stars shone brighter
I know that I still have
a place in your heart
I feel your hand in mine
when your absence
accompanies me
throughout the day
I miss you

Coastal mood ...

Rugged rocky cliffs
frame the coastline
Green pastures
perched up high
Clouds with fluff
line the horizon
Shells with broken edges
dug deep in the sand
Fish that jump
not caught in nets
Birds that dive
into deep waters of blue
Winds that blow
carrying waves to shore
Crabs walking sideways
looking for toes
Darkened skies
bring angry seas
crashing hard into
the cliffs
Sheep that graze
and look over in wonder
at all the commotion
of nature below
Moods and motions
of different scenarios
playing out
in a framed moment
painted by life

Remembering you ...

You walked
with the light
of a new day
into yesterday
A tear
still lingers
ready to fall
into tomorrow

Thank you

Thank you
for seeing me
Giving me
the gift of you
and a heart that allows
me to feel once more
If you ever cross my path again
I won't forget you and
the sparkle in your eye
will always
light my path
with a smile
knowing
I was so lucky
to meet you
It is a rare find
the gift of connection
the gift of a smile –
when I enter your space
The gift of true desire –
felt so strongly
A gift of hope
I can repay
someday
somewhere
Thankyou
I know you came to me for a reason
but you left
way too soon

Dance of the butterflies

Silently the morning light
wove its way
through the forest
lighting a golden pathway
for all to see
and follow
I wandered into this glorious
mist
and was surrounded by a cluster of
blue winged butterflies
woken by the magic
of a new day
We danced slowly to the tune
of the morning
basking in the sensuous touch
of the sunlight
and the cool morning air
Peace

The flight of your spirit

Fly like a bird
through the winds
of time
Guide your wings
through the seasons
of change
Fly high over seas
of wonder
Scale high mountains
and watch
the world below
move through its day
Silhouette against the setting sun
and sing with the voice
of a new day
when
the light of a new day wakens
Let your spirit fly
Spread your wings
and show the world
the beauty
and majesty
of you

Our paradise

The sea slips away from
the shore
as the moon disappears into
the horizon
My thoughts drift away
with the outgoing tides
and take me to
our island
in the sun

You are waiting there
in our paradise
only we can find
together

Touch of life

The sensory touch of another's hand
through the beginnings of life
to life's end
Encompassing the many levels
we engage on
we travel though
in our lives
within the many relationships we experience
to touch
to clasp
to grip
to feel
strong
gentle
weak
The energy shared
The energy valued
The energy felt
is as real as electrical energy flowing
through wiring systems
Holding hands through life
from a plumped up new little hand
to one wearing the scars of time
We hold onto life
We hold onto care
We hold onto love
We hold on to live

The invisible connection felt
as we intertwine our fingers
and hold onto and feel connected to another
A beautiful gift to treasure

Drowning

The gentle words you whisper
in my ear
The warmth of your breath that brushes past
my cheek
The soft feel of your hand as you sweep
my hair from my face
The love in your eyes that catches
my heart
I cannot explain how it makes
me feel

You drown me in a feeling so lovely
I never want to surface
The depth of our emotion is so deep
I will hold my breath for as long as
you are here

Come swim in my ocean

Stay

Silent thoughts

If I could just reach through time
If I could just retrace my steps
If I could just unfreeze my voice
If I could just look back at you and catch your stare
If I could just let you know I care
If I could just have another chance
If I could just know why you came by
If I could just once more say hi
I would be over the moon

To loved ones

To our loved ones
wherever they may be
Be they far away or close
to home
Our loved ones help make us
who we are today
They are in our dreams
They help us build our dreams
Travel roads we may not usually
venture on
Help us, make us
follow the stars and see where they lead
us
Loved ones give us our smile
Give us hope
Give us a reason to be the best
we can be
Loved ones are just that
'Loved ones'
Forever in our hearts
Forever at the end of our rainbow
Waiting for us to return
someday
To feel their love
once more
To all our loved ones
in our dreams

in our lives
across the oceans
You are loved
so loved
and remembered
and felt
always

Always with me

Night time falls
there's a touch of coolness
permeating the humid still air
A flicker of light
opens my eyes
as your hand reaches through
the veil of time and space
and draws me into your
arms
We are together in our world
of thoughts
Our safe place filled with
our shared desire
to be together
I love this place
of feeling and sensing you

Always with me

The gift

I found a gift
under the tree
It had a red bow
and a card to me
It was beautifully wrapped
with gold paper
and was square
It lit up with light
I couldn't help but stare
I unwrapped it slowly
so many layers it had
The last layer said 'I love you'
for that I am so glad
It was from you
a magical gift
with a golden glow
I held it to my heart
just so you would know
'I love you too'

My note to you

I pick up the pen
to write sweet words
to you
I thought I could never
write again
But life always blooms
where you least expect it
The ink is filled with
hope
that on another morning
when the sun casts a light
over the world
you will walk out of the shadow
of yesterday
and once again you'll
catch my heart
as it jumps onto
your path
that is scattered with
words
I have written
to you

Listen

Together
let's gently unwrap
the many layers
of our lives
until we reach
our hearts
then listen
to the raw beat
of our song
together

One more song

Just one more song
before I let you go
I'll dance with you
in my heart
The lyrics will wrap themselves
around us
and I'll move slowly with you
in my arms
Just one more song
before I say goodbye
to a special light that
walked out of my dreams
and swept my feelings
off their feet
and into your melody –
a tune forever
playing
in my mind
Just one more song
before you go

You inflame me...

Your hands
touch
with velvet feel
against my skin
Your eyes
mesmerising
gaze deep into my soul
Your heart
beats
the tune
of my heightened senses
You capture
me
in a glow
I can't comprehend
As you lead me
into the burning fire
of
my desires

A feeling of home ...

Sometimes a summer breeze
will sweep you up
within its warm heart
and carry you to a place
you feel is home
Sometimes a winter wonderland
will cool your senses
take you into your imagination
within the mists and fogs
that sit outside your window
Sometimes high up in the mountains
the view you see
is within yourself
It encapsulates all that you are
all you inspire to be
as you absorb the beauty and majesty
surrounding you
Sometimes within the ocean
the blue fluid glass
that encases you
slows down your thoughts, your presence
as you drift through a world
inspiring adventure, feats of courage,
poetry and romance

Sometimes you are carried
on a summer breeze
to a place you call
home

Shades of night ...

Saffron colours
Puffs of white
Green shades of freshness
elude the night

Seas of blue
are shades of steel
Shadows emerge
as the moon becomes real

Noises are louder
as sounds die down
Dreams take over reality
when night time comes to town

You make me sigh ...

Is it the depth
I see in your eyes
or the tenderness
I hear in your words
Is it the desire
I feel in your
presence
or the adventure
I know is in
your soul
Is it your smile
that makes me
crumble
or how I feel
when you take
my hand
Is it all your
charms
that fill my
heart
every time
I look at you
that
just
makes
me
sigh

Dividing line ...

Is it real
what I feel?
When we meet
you seem so sweet
Is it true
what I feel
for you?
I wish I was brave
then our moments
I would save
just to enjoy them again
I know the line is there
to divide us
Our lives exist on a
different bus
So we just look
out the window
and wonder
if what we feel and know
could be as nice
as it seems
when we meet on that line
and for a moment
in time
share a smile

Windows of your soul ...

Searching for eyes
that look back
Searching for eyes
that can see within
Searching for eyes
to drown myself in
Searching for eyes
that reflect the sky
So I can fly
to you

Bookmarked

I tried to turn
the page
but I just can't
My heart won't
let me
So I placed a bookmark
there
to remember
to return
when I need
to feel
again

The day you walked into ...

When you walked into my today
I couldn't believe the way
you made me feel.

When you walked into my yesterday
I can't believe the way
it makes me feel.

If you walk into my tomorrow
I believe that all my sorrow
will no longer be a part
of any day
that comes my way.

The treasure within ...

Within the blue seas
of my home
I seek the treasure
of your soul
I have been gifted
so much gold
within the years
of my journey
Golden hearts, smiles and love
But within the blue
I still seek you
who without knowing
will heal the life now
broken within my soul
If it be only for a moment
as the currents of time
encircle the earth
I will have experienced
the depth I see in your ocean
the depth I see in your eyes
the depth I feel in your heart
the depth I feel in your love
Within our days left upon the earth
I know you will surface
and the blue seas of my home
will carry you to me
within a random wave
that happens to break
upon my shore

Love is ....

Love
What a beautiful word
It covers all boundaries
spreads its wings
like a bird
It sees past our imperfections
It sees past the barriers we erect
It sees past oceans and mountains
An invisible energy we happily detect

It's the only purity we have
It sees deep into our heart
and when we are fortunate
to meet it
it's too hard to let such beauty
depart

Love is light ...

Tears like raindrops fall
and quench the thirst
of a heart in drought.
Emotion feeds your dying soul
and life once again
illuminates through your eyes.
I see your light
as it shines so bright;
a radiant aura
fuelled by the new love
placed ever so gently across
your path
for you to trip and fall into.

Love is lost
Love is found
Time heals those destined
and two hearts are bound –
together.

A moment in rhyme ....

Is there a time
Is there a space
when all that we do face
is a matter of time
A matter of moment
which will pass
as we lament
about the space in time
when you were mine
and the matter of time
was just another part
of the rhyme

Empty words

If your eyes are empty
when you talk
to me
Your words will have
no value

Connecting our thoughts

Can we travel into the unconscious world
we have yet to discover?
Can we dream in a place where our mind
cannot trace -
where no maps have direction
where direction has no meaning
where only thoughts wander in unison
until they find their destination
their reason for being formed in the mind
the answer to the reason?
Can we dream in the unconscious sphere
and enjoy all that cannot enter our
current perception
without being cognizant of what is happening
but affecting who we are
what direction we follow
who we connect with
in our supposed present awareness?
Can we? Do we?

Your library ...

When I wandered
into your life
I found myself
surrounded by a library
of stories,
a library of emotions,
a library of a life
I had never encountered.
Each book
held a fascination,
a fascination I had to read,
I had to bury my head into,
bury my heart into
to understand
the library.
The library built not for you
but of you.
It had become my world,
a world I had fallen into
to read each book
until the last page
was turned.

Autumn leaves ....

The autumn leaves are crisp and brown
winter mist lies all around
Shadows lurk in corners nearby
afraid the sunlight will reach the eye
Age that's weary from days of trying
Tears in drought from years of crying
Time marks our time as it rules our days
Memories linger in yesterday's haze
We play in groups 'The game of Life'
or wander alone on the edge of a knife
We love, we smile, we win, we lose,
we fight, we smirk at those we choose
We talk, we sing, we eat, we drink,
we run, we travel, we learn to think
We mock those we don't understand
We move in dance to the sounds of a band
The autumn leaves are brown again
and winter mists are full of rain
Time ticks on for each and all
as summer sunshine makes way for fall

Lost in your music ...

Listening to you playing
your guitar
is like you go for a wander
along my inner path
until you reach
my heart
Your beautiful words
linger there
while your tune
weaves
a magic cloak
that enshrouds me
and I am completely
lost
within your song

You give me life

The cool morning air
wrapped its arms around me
The sky was splashed with the colours
of dawn
You opened the door
of my cage
and
I flew into the sunrise

Snapshot moment

The room was hazy
with smoke imbued air
The tone of the music
was low and evocative
I felt like I was sitting
in a black and white snapshot
as your eyes caught me
off guard
and I threw back
a glance
then mulled over the sea of bodies
that lay between us
Romance now filled
the rooms smoky aura
as you wove your way
through my veins
and led me to the other side
of the moon

Silhouette of a whisper

If we could dance in the
moonlight
to music of your choice,
would you hold me close and kiss
me,
whispering sweet words with
your voice.
Could we stand in the moon light
and silhouette the scene.
Just you and me together
so loving and so serene.

The ghosts of change ....

The leaf that floats
into your hand
has travelled with ghosts
from a distant land.
It found a place
on which to rest,
the ghosts of change
time in their bodies,
none left to invest.
It's cracking frame
aged and worn,
brown and withered
and in parts, torn.
You lay it in the earth
to sleep,
the ghosts of change
into their hands, to keep.

Into you ....

If I say yes
with my eyes
will you answer
yes with your lips
If I touch
your hand gently
will your arms
enclose me
If I sigh
with love's emotion
will your heart
dance with mine
If I'm afraid
to let go
will you catch me
as I fly

Into you

A day of sunshine ...

Dreams that take you
on a boat with a mast
Over the waves
away from your past
Walking together
hand in hand
Feet sinking into
sea washed sand
Sunlit shadows
decorate the ground
Shells with feet
that make no sound
Winds that blow
and catch your hair
Moments caught
into nothing you stare
Nothing filled with something
on a horizon far way
Sailing with my soul
on a sunshine filled day

Riding horses ...

Riding horses
over blue seas of tears
Waves carrying thoughts
visions of the years
without you

Throwing caution
to the breeze
Riding horses
over the seas
to you

Shooting stars
leave trails in the sky
Riding horses with wings
Oh how I fly
with you

Riding horses
over empty plains
Riding towards
green forests of rains
feeling you

Riding horses
wild and free
Reflections painted
of you and me
together

Nature's tune ...

The creek I follow
meanders through
forests of colour
I feel leaves like rain
gently falling
around me
Carpeting the ground
in colours of gold
Softly the sounds
of branches reaching
high up into streams
of filtered sunlight
Listening to the songs
of nature
while birds in chorus
sing tunes of old
I find myself lost
in harmony
accepted into a
privileged world
All who reside here
live without
judgement
Respect for all
who maintain
the peace

Another day ...

Sunrise feelings
peace at hand
Colours cascading
all across the land
Exposing the truth
as clouds do part
Sunrise feelings
journeying through my heart
White dew layers
the earth at dawn
Young children wide eyed
greet the morning with a yawn
Soft hues of yellow
over a sky that's blue
Realising who's real
and all that is true
Sunrise feelings
greet the day
As I open the door
and go on my way

Tides ...

Just as the ocean breathes
I breathe
I rise, I fall
I'm wild, I'm still
You still can't work out
the way of the tides
because you only
swim in lakes

Fear ...

Fear sat on my
shoulders
and pushed
my head into the earth
Darkness,
lit my path
Colour,
a beautiful treat
Laughter,
a special treasure
and love,
love was the diamond
that glistened
in the shadows
just out of reach

The games you play ...

I fell into the river
you so carefully placed
at my feet
You were overjoyed to see me struggle
in the current
as I got swept away in your game
You laughed as I surfaced
and I lost my ability
to use my strength
My uncertainties
dragged me down
with the weight of your presence
The drop of the waterfall
was just ahead
Do I let the river continue
to guide me over the edge
and drown in its power
No
My silent battle continues
as I grab onto the safety of a rock
and surface -
Maintaining my dignity
My inner strength
My power

I'm back

His lonely road...

He wandered along the lonely road
and raised his eyes to the stars.
He had lost all that was his to cherish,
all but two fancy cars.

He wandered slowly on
hoping to never reach the end.
He heard his phone start ringing
and saw it was his lifelong friend.

The tears welled up in his eyes
as he spoke to his friend at length.
The friend gave him kind words of support
to help him and give him some strength.

How could he go on and see tomorrow
when today had taken his jewel.
The road was long with not much light
and his heart was low on fuel.

Along the road he found a dog,
scruffy and needing some care.
The dog came up and walked beside him,
together they made quite a pair.

So as the sun began to rise
and the road now led to home.
He carried the dog that needed some love
and now, together, they would never feel alone.

Sorry he said ...

Sorry he said
I'm so sorry
as he bowed his head
I lost the path
back to you
After all the rivers
I crossed
I hoped there was a way
through
the tears to get back
to my true
love

She cried
She cried for all the days
she waited
She found herself in a maze
lost and confused
Then through the haze
another path
caught her gaze
and led her away
from him
to you

Blurred lines ...

Focus blurred
Sharp corners
rounded
Petals frozen
in time
Lines drawn
in the sand
Crossing oceans
deep with doubt
Focus sharpened
Image distorted
Mind games
tricks
Answers unknown
Marked absent
and yet
I see

Safe haven ...

Drops of tears
flood her heart
cascading in waves
of emotion
Crashing on shores
of promised lands
Steering her heart
within the winds of time
Making sense of maps
drawn in the past
When the excitement
of discovery
was rewarded in the pleasure
of sharing the lonely frontiers
of their love
and building a
new beginning together
but
frontiers are conquered
by natural influences
of outside forces
seeking shelter
in the haven
of a heart
open
to all who admire
the false façade
of a safe place
to drop anchor

His shadow ...

Grey clouds
gather
The sun sets
without colour
Waters swirl
in an angry swell
Her smile
subsides
Her heart is encased
in protective armour
The mood
sabotages
any joy she feels
and floods the air
with antipathy
as the shadow
of his darkness
approaches

Tomorrow's light ....

Within the moonlight
I sense your guidance
as I am led
out of the darkness
into tomorrow

Etched in the sand ...

The coolness of the sea air
skims over the waves,
grabs our senses
and tingles our skin.
Memories of childhood days
and camping by the shore,
surrounded my vision.
It brings a smile to my face
and calmness to my soul.
Remembering climbing cliffs
and finding shells,
chasing crabs
as they disappear into tiny holes
in the sand.
Cuttlefish and seaweed
decorate the beach
as we stop to view the blue beauty
of the ocean.
I feel your hand in mine
and I'm at peace,
so immersed in the feeling
and the gentle sounds
of this moment.

But you too are a memory,
one that walks with me as I
follow the past footprints
etched in the sand.

Dusk ...

The orange colours of dusk
settle over the land
as I sit and watch the sun go down,
cup of tea in hand.
It colours the green and brown hues
of my home,
soaking in the natural vista
where many of us roam.
If I look closely, focus on movement
within my view,
I see a beautiful grazing mob
of our wonderful kangaroo.

Finding you, finding home ...

Tracking the winds
of your words

To find my way home

Climbing high mountains
and seeking the light
in your eyes

To find my way home

Connecting to your heart
and clasping the strings
to your soul

To find my way home

Following the currents
and hearing your music
in the roll of the waves

To find my way home

Feeling your words
like a warm hug
by the fire

I will find you again
My home

Just you and me ...

When our eyes meet
everything around us
disappears
We are in our world
that belongs to just us
No sounds
other than our voices
our heart beats
No movement
other than our smiles
For a moment
the space between us
is filled only by us
No one can enter
It's our space
Just you and me
and a feeling we can't explain
when our eyes meet

Awkward moment ...

When the time came
to say
'goodbye'
We shuffled our feet
in awkward silence
An invisible hug
was waiting to be given
But we smiled
looked down
then said our 'goodbyes'
Another time?
Maybe?

I wrote you a song ...

Have you danced
to my song
that I wrote for you

Have you listened
to my words
believe me, they're true

Have you seen
your smile
and how it lights up the room

Have you heard
your heart beat
to your beautiful tune

Have you felt
your warmth
and the calmness that you bring

Have you seen
how happy you make me –
It's you that makes my heart sing

You make me smile ...

To be in your presence
is just so easy
like walking through springtime
but with a summer feel
There are no nerves,
there is no pondering
or
worrying about what I say
There is just an easy
smile
and
you

You bring the sunshine ...

Summer days
Summer haze
Storm clouds loom
Camera on zoom
Phone call terse
Car in reverse
Trying to see
some positivity
Then your eyes light
the day
as you walk my way
and I say
'hey'
It's good to see you
again

The crinkle of your smile ...

Is it the crinkle
at the corner of your mouth
when you smile
or
the twinkle
in your eye
in the sunlight
or
the little looks
you give
and catch me
doing the same

Whatever it is
all together –
it just melts my heart

You ...

Your soul
is as graceful
as a wish on the breeze
and all who are touched by it
find a home forever in your heart

Your wings
are like the lace of a beautiful
dream
woven together
with threads of love

Your voice
is like the gentleness
of a creek in flow
quietly guided to ears
open to your sound

Your eyes
attract all who catch their gaze
Windows of beauty
always open to those
who can see
'you'

Every time ...

Every time the music plays
I think of you
and our summer days
I think of you
you're all I see
the music plays
so beautifully

Every time the words I hear
hold hands with notes
ever so clear
The music plays
our summer days
My summer days
with you

Let the music play ...

While the music keeps playing
and your body keeps swaying
I'm just saying
it's worth staying
in a place
that fills your space
and puts a smile on your face
within a sense or a sound
that lifts you off the ground
and makes you feel
good

If life just gave me you ...

If life just gave us friendship
I would feel so blessed to have you
as my friend
If life just connected us with a thread of hope
I would never let it go
If life just gave us a smile to keep
your smile would always be etched
within my sight
If life gave us love to share
I would never erase the feeling of you
from my heart
If life just gave us one last dance
I would hold you so close under the light of the moon
and never let the music stop playing
If life just ...

Floating on thoughts of you ...

Above the clouds
I watch the world go by
Up here in the silence
of a pale blue sky

We fly up here
a plane going somewhere
Leaving a line of white cloud
as we streak through the air

I wonder if you walk the street
once happily shared by both our feet
I wonder if when you look above
you think about a heart so full of love

If I look down below many things pass by
Mountains so green and pastures of gold
The red soil of our land
embracing ancestors of old

Writing these words
in a bubble full of others
Sounds of many voices
Children and their mothers

All going somewhere
it may take a little time
Flying high in the wide blue yonder
listening to music and trying to rhyme

We cross over the coast
White sandy beaches, a playground for many
Turquoise waters
the colour of your eyes, so uncanny

My mind drifts off
in the beauty below
as boats and ships sail the waters
with their nautical dreams in tow

I always think of you
in the quiet times of my life
You take my mind away
to a place free of noise, anger and strife

I just imagine your smile
and how it makes my day
as I float above the clouds
and am heading your way

Sometimes we feel lost ...

Sometimes
we lose sight
of our world
Sink like a stone
into the ocean
of self-doubt
We drop
down
down
Not letting our instinct
guide us back
to the surface
We hold our breath
our courage
Our fears grip tightly
Shadows watch us
Conditioning monitors our habits

We sink like a stone
into other's oceans
and flow within their currents
until we break free
swim to the surface
and
breathe
Feel the sun again
and see the blue sky
once more

Understanding despair ...

Maybe one day
you'll understand
When the hand you hold
is cold
When the lips you kiss
lack softness
When the eyes you look into
have no depth
When the voice you hear
has no warmth
When you long to know
that, that smile is for you
When you long to know
that your life has some meaning
When the love you long to feel
is out of reach
Maybe one day you'll understand
and realise
when you long to unlock the door
of winter
and feel the freshness and beauty
of springtime
once again

Reminders and memories ...

Foot prints left
upon the shore
People come and go
now no more
Coincidences
take me back in time
Memories of feelings
when for a moment
you were mine
I open up pages
and there you are again
Renewing my memories
like fresh life after rain
No matter how many footprints
are left on the land
Each day a new reminder
that yours still remain in the sand

Drought ...

My dried out body is ready to crumble
as my roots can no longer find the moisture
they seek to quench my ever present thirst
from the red parched earth we are a part of.
My limbs will crack and fall into the drying sands.
I am dying under the clear blue skies and
yellow scorching sun,
a slow sad death
shared by any life form in our vast surrounds.
I have tried in vain to hold on to life
but with no rains,
all who share this land,
all who fight the soldiers of drought,
remain in battle
until hope becomes despair
and the life blood of our land
flows into distant memories.

One day our life will reform
as our dormant seeds soak in the new rains
that will fall in future days
and once again life and colour will return
to this arid land –
this is our circle of our existence ..

The journey through a book ...

If I open a book
and follow its pathway
through the many pages
in front of me.
I find myself in all sorts of places,
with all sorts of people.
I may reach the other end
full of information
with which I can 'conquer the world'
or I may witness the beginnings
of a beautiful relationship.
I may also experience great sadness,
adventure, sail the high seas,
as I wander through the world of words
that paints pictures in my mind;
a world that may be real
or a world discovered by the author
of the book.
As my journey ends
I feel enriched for the experience
I just wandered through
and a sense of sadness
that this adventure, romance, plethora
of information
is now over for me
but I'm sure the next traveller
will discover the treasure chest
of words

that will make their experience
a pathway worth their visit
and time well spent in these books
we often escape into.
We learn, we love, we laugh,
we ponder, we question,
we travel
and we discover.
Read.

Just nearby ...

I walk beside you everyday
but you don't see me
I hold your hand
when you feel fear
but you don't feel it
I laugh and smile at your jokes
but you don't hear me
I wipe your tears when you're sad
but you don't know it
I'm always there for you
because I love you
You just don't realise it
One day you will

Remembrance Day

Silently
as raindrops fall.
Tears from heaven
for all
those who gave
their lives
for us.
Over the years
many conflicts
fought.
Arriving home
and many fraught
with scars
we will never understand.
Memories
that remain within,
trauma experienced,
loss of friends, limbs and kin.
Care for those
who cared enough for
you
to leave the safety
of their home
not knowing if they
will ever roam
free again
but
you do.

Bring back some magic ...

Let's bring back magic
into our lives
Let's be the reason
of the twinkle in other's eyes
Let's share our smiles
with those who are down
Let's laugh
at our imperfections
instead of judgement
with a frown
Let's enjoy any people and gifts
that come our way
Let's just try to live our best
however we spend our day.
Let's bring back magic
into our lives
Remember what it was like to be a child
when super heroes and imagination
were the stars in our eyes

Let's get lost together ...

Your hand
slips into mine
so easily
Tingles
of nervousness
pulsate
throughout me
I stare
into you
as you draw me
into
your beautiful aura
We dance
on your breath
as it swirls
magically
around us
Your lips
like gentle cushions
of emotion
throw mine
into disarray
as I disappear
into a world
I have just begun
to journey into
with you -
Let's get lost

Who needs words ...

The conversation between
our eyes
is so intense
no one else can intrude
It's a language
only we understand
and get lost in

Our silent conversation
that is louder
than
any vocal words

I love having this conversation
with you

The voice of silence ...

Silence speaks
in shallow footsteps
no more heard
upon my path

I see you still
within my sight
Your portrait hangs
within my mind

Silence speaks
in words not spoken
Your last look
I turned away
Forgive me

Letting go ...

I have to move on
it's time to let go
This hurts me so much
more than you know
The wisps of time
are carrying me away
through the vortex of missing you
into a new day

Thinking of you ...

I wrote you a song
within the melody of notes
and placed it
on the wing of a breeze
as it passed through my heart
on its way
to find you

Into the blue ...

I don't know where the wind will guide
me
as it plays tenderly with my hair
I don't know where the waves will
carry me
following the currents to somewhere
I know the blue entices me,
always lost within its hue
maybe the winds and waves understand
it's where I think I'll find,
my real you

Broken hearts ...

So many broken hearts
scattered like autumn leaves
on paths we walk on
The winter winds may blow
them out of sight
but they still lie broken
somewhere else
and
cold days bring no joy
as hearts need warmth
to gel and mend
So many broken hearts
need fixing
Hopefully spring rains
will feed the seeds
and
love will bloom for those
needing a hug
and
a bit of special super glue
to make the heart
feel whole once more

Finally ...

Peering through my
sunglasses
into the yellow glow
of the day
a silhouette appears
in my vision
and it comes my way
As it moves closer
I focus on what I can see,
a familiar walk and smile
it's you, it's you
Now it's our time to be -
just you
and
me

Looking back

It's amazing looking back
to see how far you've come,
to see if you have danced with the wind
or followed the path of the sun.

It's amazing looking back
at the space that lies between,
from a place where you first stood in wonder
to how you've grown and what you've seen.

With the sun at your back
and the time that you now face,
one wonders what and who now lies in wait;
what life will gift you in this space.

And as the past melts into each night,
the days to come
are yet within our sight,
I sit in wonder at all that I've done
from my very first smile,
to always appreciating, the rising sun.

The gift of time ...

Is there enough time?
I don't know
One minute we are children
playing in the field
with freedom blowing through
our hair
and sun kissed smiles
as we chase our friends or
climb trees looking out into forever
Next, we are blushing at the boy
on the train
or kissing with gusto
the crush we had at school
Gifts and cards we've kept
that make us smile at the memory
Photos of fun days when being carefree
with backpacks was all we
cared about
Next thing life is staring at us
Our dreams are floating away
within the clouds above
Is there enough time?
We all say there is,
then all of a sudden we are given
one more chapter to read.
The childhood days,
the teenage woes and woos,
the years of freedom, exploring
and digging for that treasure

that will make our lives worthwhile,
the children we produce and adore –
we now look back at
Everything has a limit, a time,
a tide to catch,
either into shore or out to sea
The tides of time are ours
until life decides
our fate and we are carried
away into the mystery of why
Is there enough time?
Don't measure it,
roll with it while the air you breathe
still fills your lungs
and your heart still flutters
at all the things that you enjoy
and all the people
you love
That's what it's all about,
no matter how much time
we have

I will find you in your
eyes
for that's where your
truth lies

- ailsa craig

My beautiful Dad and I many moons ago

Other poetry books written by Ailsa Craig in this series